WRITER'S
TOOLBOX

W9-BDF-167

Action!
Writing Your Own Play

by **Nancy Loewen**

illustrated by
Dawn Beacon

PICTURE WINDOW BOOKS
a capstone imprint

Editor: Jill Kalz
Designer: Nathan Gassman
Production Specialist: Jane Klenk
The illustrations in this book were created with acrylics.

Picture Window Books
151 Good Counsel Drive
P.O. Box 669
Mankato, MN 56002-0669
877-845-8392
www.capstonepub.com

J808.2
LOE
402-8687

All books published by Picture Window Books
are manufactured with paper containing at least
10 percent post-consumer waste.

Library of Congress Cataloging-in-Publication Data
Loewen, Nancy, 1964–
 Action! : writing your own play / by Nancy Loewen ; illustrated
by Dawn Beacon.
   p. cm. — (Writer's toolbox)
 Includes index.
 ISBN 978-1-4048-6017-9 (library binding)
 ISBN 978-1-4048-6392-7 (paperback)
 1. Playwriting—Juvenile literature. I. Title.
 PN1661.L54 2010
 808.2—dc22
                  2010000886

Printed in the United States of America in North Mankato, Minnesota.
042011
006171R

Special thanks to our adviser,
Terry Flaherty, PhD, Professor of English,
Minnesota State University, Mankato,
for his expertise.

People in colorful costumes sing and dance across the stage. Music fills the air. Lights blaze and dim. You feel like you're in a different world.

Whether performed on Broadway or in a school gym, all plays begin the same way. They begin with a story. They begin with someone putting words on a page. And YOU can be that someone!

Read the following play, *It's My Name Too!* Then go back to page 5 and start learning about the tools you need to write your own play.

Here's a summary of the play in this book:

It's My Name Too! by Nancy Loewen

John Jacob Jingleheimer Schmidt lives in Tale Town. A man moves in next door with the same long, funny name. This causes confusion in town. The men enjoy the attention they get for their name and don't want to share. They flip a coin to decide who gets to keep the name. The newcomer wins, but when he sees how sad his neighbor is, he offers to share the name. The two become friends.

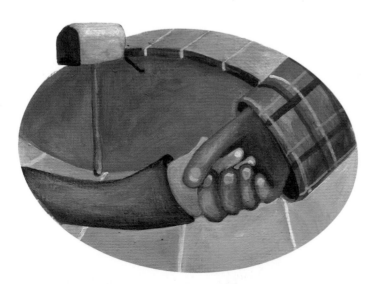

~ Tool 1 ~

A play should have people, animals, or creatures who are trying to solve a problem. It should have a **PLOT**. A plot is a series of events that are connected to each other. One event leads to another. There is a beginning, a middle, and an end.

~ Tool 2 ~

Writing a play will be easier if you **PLAN** your story before you start writing. It helps to have the ending in mind. (Remember, you can always change things later.)

5

Cast of Characters for

It's My Name Too!

JOHN
(John Jacob Jingleheimer Schmidt) (a big guy)

POSTMASTER PEGGY
(a bit scatterbrained)

TOWNSPERSON 1

TOWNSPERSON 2

TOWNSPERSON 3

JACOB

(the other John Jacob Jingleheimer Schmidt) (a little guy)

TOWNSPERSON 4

LITTLE BOY

LITTLE BOY'S MOM

~ Tool 3 ~

Most plays have **MAIN CHARACTERS** and **MINOR CHARACTERS**. Main characters are the ones the story is about. The main characters in this play are John and Jacob. But minor characters are important too. They might not have many lines (or even have names), but they give the main characters something to react to.

~ Tool 4 ~

A list of everyone in the play is called the **CAST OF CHARACTERS**. If you want, you can add a short description of each character.

~ Tool 5 ~

Plays are divided into **SCENES**. A scene is a part of the story that happens in one time and place. When the location changes, or to show time has passed, you'll need to start a new scene. In this play, scene 1 takes place in front of Jacob's and John's houses.

~ Tool 6 ~

STAGE DIRECTIONS are put in parentheses. These words are never spoken. They tell the actors how to move or how to say their lines. Stage directions explain details that the audience will see and hear when the play is performed.

SCENE 1

(A sidewalk in front of JACOB's new house. JACOB is moving in. He is carrying a stack of boxes so tall he can barely see over them. JOHN lives next door. He comes out of his house, looking at a newspaper. He isn't paying attention to where he's going. The two bump into each other.)

~ Tool 7 ~

DIALOGUE is what characters say to each other. It's what a play is all about! Through dialogue, we learn what the characters are like and what they want.

~ Tool 8 ~

DIALOGUE TAGS tell the reader who is speaking. The names should be in capital letters so they stand apart from other words. Here, both main characters have the same name. That could be confusing! So the dialogue tags in this play will be "JOHN" (the Tale Town native) and "JACOB" (the newcomer).

JOHN: Sorry! Didn't see you there. Are you new in town?

(JACOB puts down the boxes and shakes JOHN'S hand.)

JACOB: Sure am. My name is John—

JOHN: (excited) Hey, so is mine.

JACOB: Jacob—

JOHN: No kidding! Me too!

JACOB: Jingleheimer—

JOHN: (his excitement fading) I can't believe this.

JACOB: Schmidt.

JOHN: Oh, no.

(They stop shaking hands and glare at each other.)

(TOWNSPERSON 1 and TOWNSPERSON 2 walk by.)

TOWNSPERSON 1: Good morning, John Jacob Jingleheimer Schmidt!

JOHN and JACOB: (together) Good morning!

TOWNSPERSON 2: What?! (points to JACOB) You mean YOUR name is John Jacob Jingleheimer Schmidt too?

JACOB: It most certainly is.

TOWNSPERSON 1: That's too funny. (to TOWNSPERSON 2) Isn't that just too funny? (They exit.)

(JACOB, frowning, picks up his boxes and puts them on his porch. JOHN, also frowning, goes to his own porch and paces. After a while, he returns.)

JOHN: I know you're new in town, and I don't want to be rude, but I'm not sharing my name. It's who I am!

JACOB: Who YOU are! What about who I am?

JOHN: Everyone in Tale Town knows my name. Little children grow up SINGING my name!

JACOB: I'm John Jacob Jingleheimer Schmidt. The one and only!

JOHN and JACOB: (together) I WON'T give it up!

(They stick their noses in the air, and each man goes into his house.)

~ Tool 9 ~

When people talk in real life, they aren't perfectly still. They stand, sit, move their heads and hands, and walk around. They pick things up and put them down. A play, too, should include **MOVEMENT** to keep the audience interested. Here we see John and Jacob pace, move boxes, walk across the stage, and point their noses in the air.

SCENE 2

(A few days later. JOHN is pruning a shrub. JACOB is painting his house. POSTMASTER PEGGY enters, carrying a bag of mail.)

POSTMASTER PEGGY: Good morning, John Jacob Jingleheimer Schmidt. (She hands JOHN a stack of mail.) Here's your mail.

JOHN: Thanks, Postmaster Peggy. (He flips through the mail and pulls out a magazine.) Wait—this isn't mine. I don't get *Cuckoo Clock Collector* magazine.

POSTMASTER PEGGY: (giggles) Oh my, that's an "oopsie."

(She grabs the magazine and goes next door to JACOB's house.)

POSTMASTER PEGGY: Here's your mail, John Jacob Jingleheimer Schmidt.

JACOB: Thank you, Postmaster Peggy. (He flips through the mail and pulls out a catalog.) Wait—this isn't mine. I'm not on the "Big and Tall" mailing list.

(POSTMASTER PEGGY grabs JACOB's arm and tugs him toward JOHN. The TOWNSPEOPLE, LITTLE BOY, and LITTLE BOY'S MOM enter and gather around.)

POSTMASTER PEGGY: (talking to both JOHN and JACOB) OK, this same-name business just won't do! It's too confusing. You need two different names.

JACOB: But what can we do?

LITTLE BOY: Have a contest!

JOHN: (waves his shears at JACOB) Good idea. A pruning contest.

JACOB: (shakes his head and waves his paintbrush at JOHN) No, a painting contest.

(JOHN shakes his head.)

TOWNSPERSON 3: Arm wrestling! Or a chili cook-off!

(JOHN and JACOB shake their heads.)

POSTMASTER PEGGY: Oh, for heaven's sake! If neither of you will budge, let's flip a coin. I've got a quarter right here.

JOHN: (to JACOB) Fine. Heads I win, tails you win.

(JACOB shrugs. POSTMASTER PEGGY flips the coin, and JOHN catches it.)

POSTMASTER PEGGY: (looking over JOHN's shoulder) Tails!

JACOB: (jumping excitedly) Yes! The name is mine! I'm the one and only John Jacob Jingleheimer Schmidt! (to JOHN) And you are ...

JOHN: (sad) Umm ... looks like I'm just plain old John Schmidt.

~ Tool 10 ~

Most plays, especially funny ones, make use of **EXAGGERATION.** When writers exaggerate, they make things sound bigger and better (or smaller and worse) than in real life. Having two men in town with the same name isn't just confusing, it's a disaster! Jacob isn't just pleased to keep his name. He's thrilled!

~ Tool 11 ~

When you write a play, think about the **SCENERY** and **PROPS** for each scene. Painted hangings, wooden cutouts, and walls are examples of scenery. Props are the objects that bring the scenery to life, such as magazines or coins.

Scenery and props don't have to be fancy. In this scene, cardboard could be painted to look like store shelves (scenery). The actors could carry shopping baskets or bags (props). That's enough to tell the audience that the scene takes place in a grocery store.

Spinach SALE

SCENE 3

(A few days later. A grocery store. JOHN sees JACOB and hunches over, awkwardly trying to hide behind some shelves. LITTLE BOY is in the store with his MOM.)

LITTLE BOY: (pointing to JACOB) Look, Mom, it's John Jacob Jingleheimer Schmidt!

MOM: Why, so it is. (goes up to JACOB) Hi there, John Jacob Jingleheimer Schmidt!

(Still trying to hide, JOHN cringes at the sound of his old name.)

JACOB: Oh, hello!

(MOM spies JOHN and points.)

MOM: And look, it's John Ja— ... it's John!

(JOHN is startled and straightens up. JACOB sees him now.)

JOHN: (embarrassed) I was just leaving. I think I left my coffeepot on.

(He leaves, knocking over some cookies.)

Apples 50¢

Oranges 40¢

~ Tool 12 ~

Whether your play is funny or serious, your audience will care more about the story if your characters show their **EMOTIONS**. If John didn't care so deeply about his name, there wouldn't be much of a story. And it's better to *show* emotion than to talk about it. In this scene, when John stops jogging, we understand that he's feeling sad.

Afternoon John!

SCENE 4

(JOHN and JACOB are jogging in the park. JACOB is ahead. TOWNSPERSON 3 and TOWNSPERSON 4 are also jogging, but in the other direction.)

TOWNSPERSON 4: (passing JACOB) Good afternoon, John Jacob Jingleheimer Schmidt! (passing JOHN) Afternoon, John.

TOWNSPERSON 3: (passing JACOB) Great day for a jog, isn't it, John Jacob Jingleheimer Schmidt! (passing JOHN) Afternoon, John.

(JOHN stops jogging and walks. He hangs his head. JACOB looks back at him a few times before they both exit the stage.)

SCENE 5

(JACOB paces on his porch, thinking. After a few moments he walks over to JOHN's house and knocks on his door.)

JOHN: (opening door) What do YOU want?

JACOB: Well, John, I've been thinking. Tale Town IS big enough for two John Jacob Jingleheimer Schmidts.

JOHN: (unsure) Really? But what about the mail?

JACOB: Postmaster Peggy will just have to learn to sort our mail by our house numbers. And if she gets it wrong, who cares? I'll give you yours, and you'll give me mine.

JOHN: (brightening) Are you sure?

JACOB: Yes! It's no fun being John Jacob Jingleheimer Schmidt all by myself. My name—excuse me, OUR name—should make people smile. Including you!

JOHN: (hugging JACOB) Oh, thank you! Thank you, thank you, thank you!

~ Tool 13 ~

The **CLIMAX** of a play (and any story) comes when the problem is solved. All of the story's events have been added up, and the climax is the result. In this scene, Jacob has had a change of heart. The two enemies are now friends.

23

~ Tool 14 ~

The end of the play is the **CONCLUSION.** The conclusion takes the story just a little farther than the climax. It brings the story to a satisfying end. All is well in Tale Town!

SCENE 6

(JOHN and JACOB walk through town, singing loudly. The TOWNSPEOPLE, LITTLE BOY, and LITTLE BOY'S MOM are in small groups on the stage.)

JOHN: John Jacob Jingleheimer Schmidt!

JACOB: His name is my name too!

JOHN and JACOB: (together) Whenever we go out, the people always shout ...

ALL: There goes John Jacob Jingleheimer Schmidt! La La La La La La La ... (The song repeats as the actors leave the stage.)

So, you've finished writing your play. Now what?

Take your work to the stage! First, decide who will play each character. Then have everyone read through the play to get used to his or her lines. Next comes "blocking." That's when you figure out where the actors should stand and what they should do.

Now pull the details together. What will your characters wear? What props will they use? What kind of scenery do you need? Do you need special lighting? How about music or sound effects?

A practice run, or dress rehearsal, will help your play go smoothly. You'll perform the play from start to finish, but without an audience. This will give you a chance to change anything that's not working well.

Finally, it's show time!
The words you wrote—
the story you pictured in
your mind—will come
alive onstage.

Break a leg!

(That's an old showbiz
saying. It's just a way to
say GOOD LUCK!)

Let's Review!

These are the **14 tools** you need to write a great play.

A play's **PLOT (1)** should include a problem and have a beginning, a middle, and an end. Writing a play will be easier if you **PLAN (2)** your story ahead of time. When you know your story, make a list of the **MAIN CHARACTERS** and **MINOR CHARACTERS (3)**. This list is called the **CAST OF CHARACTERS (4)**. Divide your story into **SCENES (5)**. Every scene should move the story forward. Include **STAGE DIRECTIONS (6)** to show actors how to move and speak. **DIALOGUE (7)** is what your characters say to each other. Through dialogue, the story unfolds. **DIALOGUE TAGS (8)** show which character says which lines. **MOVEMENT (9)** makes the characters seem more natural onstage. **EXAGGERATION (10)** overstates something and draws attention to it. The setting of a play, and the things that bring that setting to life, are the **SCENERY** and **PROPS (11)**. Stories are more interesting if they involve the characters' **EMOTIONS (12)**. The point in the play when the problem is solved is the **CLIMAX (13)**. Shortly afterward, the **CONCLUSION (14)** brings the play to a satisfying end.

Getting Started Exercises

- Get together with your friends. Have each person make up a character. Jot down everything you can think of about that character. Then share your characters with each other. What would happen if these characters were stuck on an island? Or competing in a dance contest? Or running for president?

- Ask your parents or teachers for some magazines. Cut out pictures of people who look interesting to you. Then cut out pictures of places, such as a sunny beach or rainy city street. See what pops into your head when you pair the people with the places.

- Sometimes it's easier to make things up as you go. Get a group of friends together. Then gather as many dress-up clothes and props as you can find. Just have fun and get silly. A story might come out of it! You can act out your idea first and write it down later. Then you can repeat your play whenever you want, or share it with other kids.

Writing Tips

Keep your dialogue short and natural-sounding. If one person talks too long, the speed of the play will slow down. The audience might lose interest.

If you get stuck, try writing character sketches. Write down everything you can think of about your characters. Really get to know them. This material won't be in the play, but it will help you create better dialogue.

If you're writing a play about history or a real experience, remember that you don't have to follow the truth exactly. You can make small changes to improve the story.

When you're done with a first draft of your play, find some people to read it out loud. Don't read yourself—just listen and take notes. Hearing your play will give you a better idea of what's working well and what isn't.

Glossary

Broadway—an area in New York City famous for its many theaters

cast—a group of actors

character—a person, animal, or creature in a story

climax—a story's most exciting moment

conclusion—an ending

detail—a piece of information, a small part of a bigger thing

dialogue—the words spoken between two or more characters

dialogue tag—the name of the character speaking, written in capital letters

emotion—a feeling, such as anger, fear, or happiness

exaggeration—overstating or going beyond the truth

line—the words an actor speaks

pace—to walk back and forth steadily

plot—what happens in a story

prop—any object used in a play that isn't scenery or costume; short for *property*

scene—a part of a story that happens in one time and place

scenery—the background or surroundings of a certain place

sound effect—any sound in a play that's not dialogue or music

stage direction—a note, in parentheses, that tells an actor how to move or speak; it also explains what appears on the stage

summary—a short version of something; giving only the main points

To Learn More

More Books to Read

Chanda, Justin, ed. *Acting Out: Six One-Act Plays! Six Newbery Stars!* New York: Atheneum Books for Young Readers, 2008.

Jacobs, Paul DuBois, and Jennifer Swender. *Putting on a Play: Drama Activities for Kids.* Salt Lake City: Gibbs Smith, 2005.

Ziefert, Harriet. *Lights on Broadway: A Theatrical Tour from A to Z.* Maplewood, N.J.: Blue Apple Books, 2009.

Internet Sites

FactHound offers a safe, fun way to find Internet sites related to this book. All of the sites on FactHound have been researched by our staff.

Here's all you do:
Visit *www.facthound.com*
FactHound will fetch the best sites for you!

Index

Look for all of the books in the Writer's Toolbox series:

Action! Writing Your Own Play
Art Panels, BAM! Speech Bubbles, POW! Writing Your Own Graphic Novel
It's All About You: Writing Your Own Journal
Just the Facts: Writing Your Own Research Report
Make Me Giggle: Writing Your Own Silly Story

Once Upon a Time: Writing Your Own Fairy Tale
Share a Scare: Writing Your Own Scary Story
Show Me a Story: Writing Your Own Picture Book
Sincerely Yours: Writing Your Own Letter
Words, Wit, and Wonder: Writing Your Own Poem